Giant Sticker Activity
Work Book

In this book you can:

Look for more than
600 stickers

Practice writing letters
and numbers

Learn to draw animals
and things that go

Sort and recognize
shapes and colors

start

 A A A

start

 a a

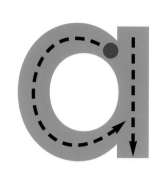 a

apple

How many ants
are there here?
Write your
answer below.

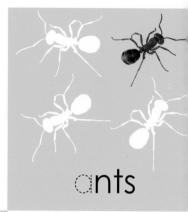
ants

What 'A' do you
breathe?

A _ _

bat

rabbit

leaf

start

B B B

start

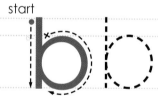 b b b

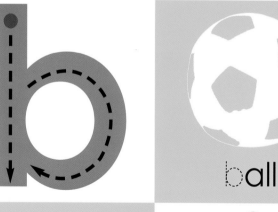 b

ball

brush

baby

What 'B' would you
wear on your feet?

B _ _ _ _ _

bag

Circle all of the 'b's.

b   d   b

d   p   b

p   d   b

bib

C c C c
start

C

car

cupcake

What 'C' would you keep as a pet?

C _ _ _

clock

What time does the clock say?

_____ o'clock

crayons

start

D D

d d

start

d

die

digger

What 'D' is it at night?

D _ _ _ _

dinosaur

What is the highest number on a die?

ducks

start

E E E

start

e e e

e

egg

What do you do when you are hungry?

E _ _ _

beetle

elephant

start

F F F

start

f f f

f

frog

flower

What 'F' can you make with your hand?

F _ _ _ _

fish

feet

fruit

G g

start
G

start
g

g

gray

gold

green

girls

goat

What 'G' is something you play?

G _ _ _ _

big rig

start
H h

start
h h

h

hat

horses

What 'H' is the opposite of 'cold'?

H _ _ _

helicopter

house

How many horses are there? Write your answer here.

start I I

start i i

ice cream

tricycles

What 'I' is in a pen?

I _ _

sick

Ian and

Tim are

twins

start J J

start j j

juice

What 'J' can make you laugh?

J _ _ _ _

jacket

jump

start K k start k k

k

keys

kittens

What 'K' can you do to a ball?

K _ _ _ _

king

Which objects unlock doors? Write your answer here.

kite

start L start l

l

Which letter do these objects begin with?

snail

ball

What 'L' is part of your mouth?

L _ _ _

drill

lion

M M

m m

motorcycle

moon

moth

What 'M' is the fifth month?

M _ _

muffin

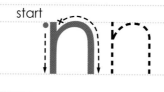

lemon

Cross out the letter that is not an 'm'.

m m m
m w m

N N

n n

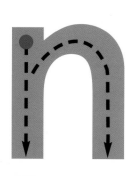

onion

nails

nine

What 'N' is used to catch fish?

N _ _

swan

Draw lines to connect the 'n's.

m   u   n
n   w   n

start O o

start O o

spoons

What 'O' is the opposite of new?

O _ _

oranges

Which birds' names begin with 'O'?

start P P

start p p

paints

purple

pink

What 'P' can you play a tune on?

P _ _ _ _ _

peas

Circle the 'p's.

p d o
o p p

pig

Q q

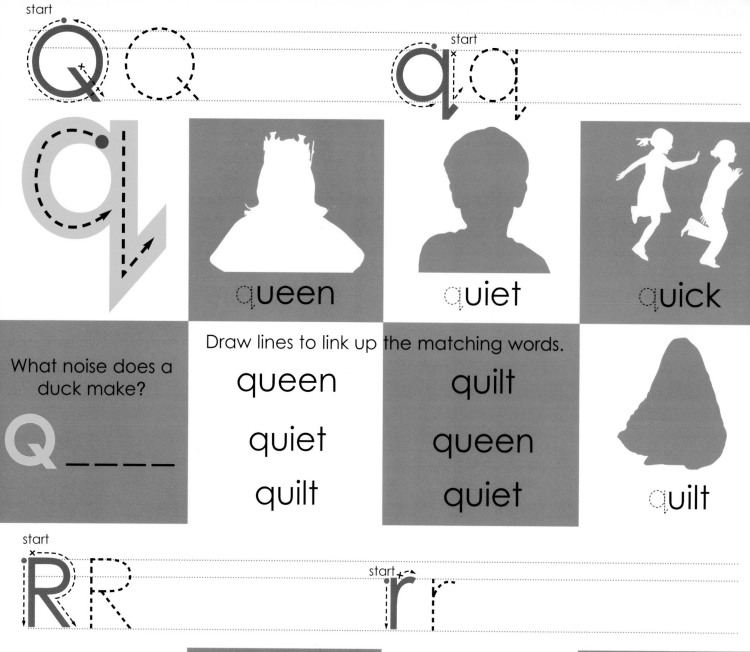

queen

quiet

quick

What noise does a duck make?

Q _ _ _ _ _

Draw lines to link up the matching words.

queen   quilt

quiet   queen

quilt   quiet

quilt

R r

How many rain drops can you count? Write your answer here.

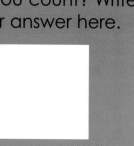

rain

rattle

What 'R' do cars drive on?

R _ _ _ _

rose

Circle the words that end in 'r'.

butter

paper

animal

rainbow

S S

S S

starfish

snake

What 'S' is an animal with a shell?

S

_ _ _ _

Add the letter 's' to these words.

cat

dog

hen

sandwich

scissors

T T

t t

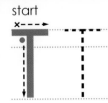

two

ten

twenty

tiger

What 'T' is the opposite of 'bottom'?

T _ _

train

462

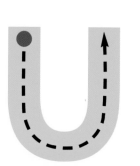

 undress

 duck

What 'U' is married to your aunt?

U_ _ _ _ _

 cup

umbrella

Circle the words tha begin with 'u'.

under   bird

crab   up

ugly   egg

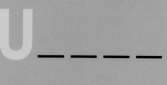

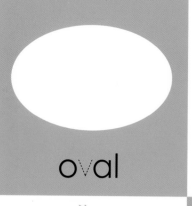 oval

vet

What 'V' do you sing with?

V_ _ _ _ _

 vase

vegetables

 violin

W w W W

W w W W

W

saw

wolf

What 'W' do you find on an airplane?

W _ _ _

watch

wheelbarrow

wheel

X x X

X x X

X

box

Which word does not end with 'x'? Write your answer here.

What 'X' means 'Christmas'?

X _ _ _

x-ray

fox

socks

Y Y Y

y y y

y

yo-yo

yawn

yellow

What 'Y' is
12 months long?

Y _ _ _ _

Circle the things that begin with 'y'.

Z Z Z

Z Z Z

Z

In which 'Z' could
you find animals?

Z _ _ _

zigzag

zebra

Sticker alphabet

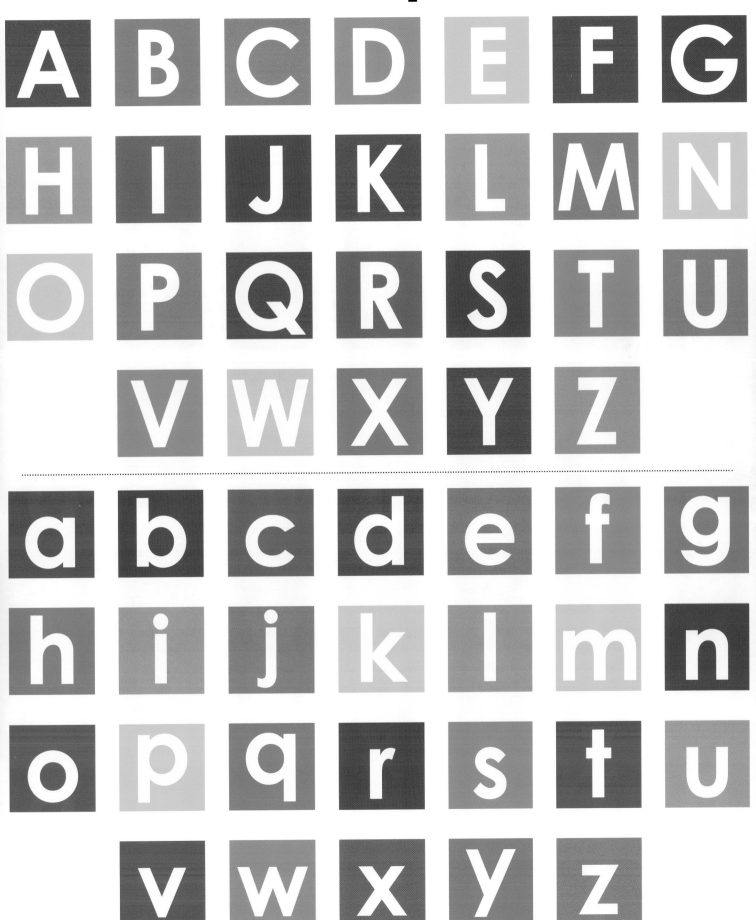

i i i i

sheepdog   harvester   hen   hay bale

donkey   barn   pig

Find the stickers of the animals and other things that belong on the farm.

one one

foal   sheep   calf   duck

cow   duckling   horse   lamb

Find the stickers of the animals, then match the babies to their moms.

2 2 2

lemons

strawberries

bananas

apples

Find the missing fruits. How many fruits are there altogether?

two two

How many cherries are there?

How many melon slices are there?

Find the stickers of things with TWO legs.

Find the two missing fruits. What are they?

start
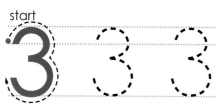

3 3 3

emergency vehicles

trucks

tractors

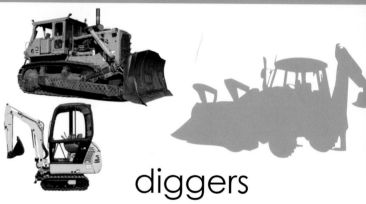

diggers

three three

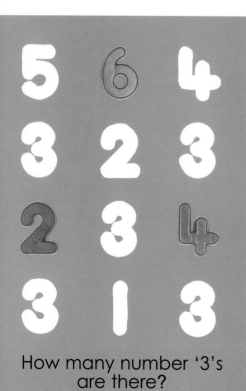

How many number '3's are there?

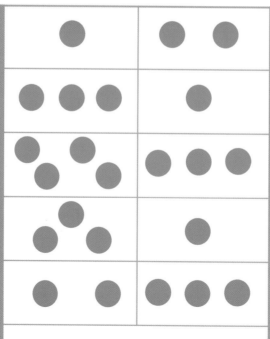

Circle the groups of three dots.

Find the three-sided shapes. What are they called?

start

4   4   4

What colors are the missing dresses?

Find the boy with the red hat.

How many presents are missing?

What colors are the missing balloons?

four four

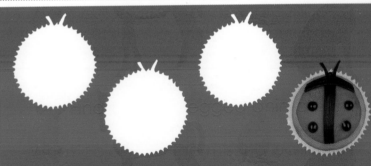

How many popsicles are missing?

How many cupcakes are there?

How many candies are blue?

Find the four-legged animals.

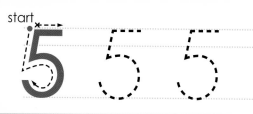

start

5 5 5

red yachts

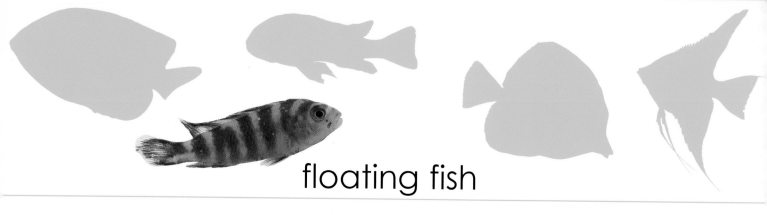

floating fish

five five

How many points does each missing star have?

How many yellow chicks are there?

5 5
1
4 2
5
2
3
5
4 5 5

How many number '5's are there?

start

6 6 6

Find the missing frogs.

Find the missing butterflies.

Find the missing dragonflies.

How many snakes altogether?

six six

How many ladybugs have six spots?

Find the bugs with six legs.

How many legs do bees have?

start

7 7 7 7

girls

boys

seven seven

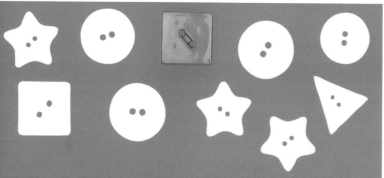

How many yellow buttons are there?

How many hats are there?

Circle the number '7's on the clocks.

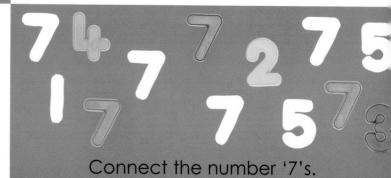

Connect the number '7's.

start

8 8 8

puppies

kittens

chicks

eight eight

Which toy has eight legs?

How many green things are there?

How many birds
are there altogether?

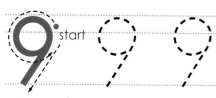

start

coins

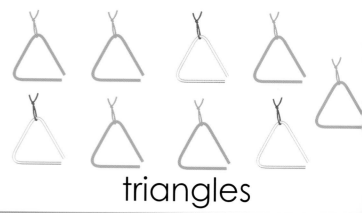

triangles

decorations

gift bows

nine nine

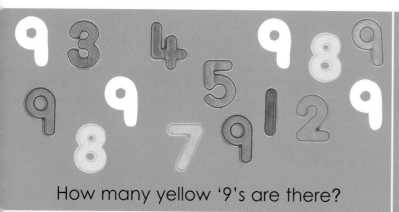

How many yellow '9's are there?

How many flowers are there?

Find the t-shirts with number '9's.

ants

die

ABC stickers

T

queen

bug

jump

C

horse

muffin

orange

K

leaf, lime and log

leaf

q

ice cream

fish

ball

kitten

kitten

brush

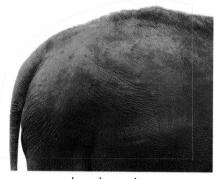

elephant

big rig

digger

ABC stickers

lemon

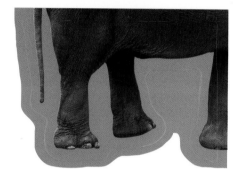

orange

crayon

hat

elephant

snail

vegetables

bat

girls

flower

bag

L

d

cupcake

ABC stickers

tricycle

scissors

king

lion

g

motorcycle

ball

fruit

ducks

goat

o

s

drill

kite

clock

sick

u

x

N

juice

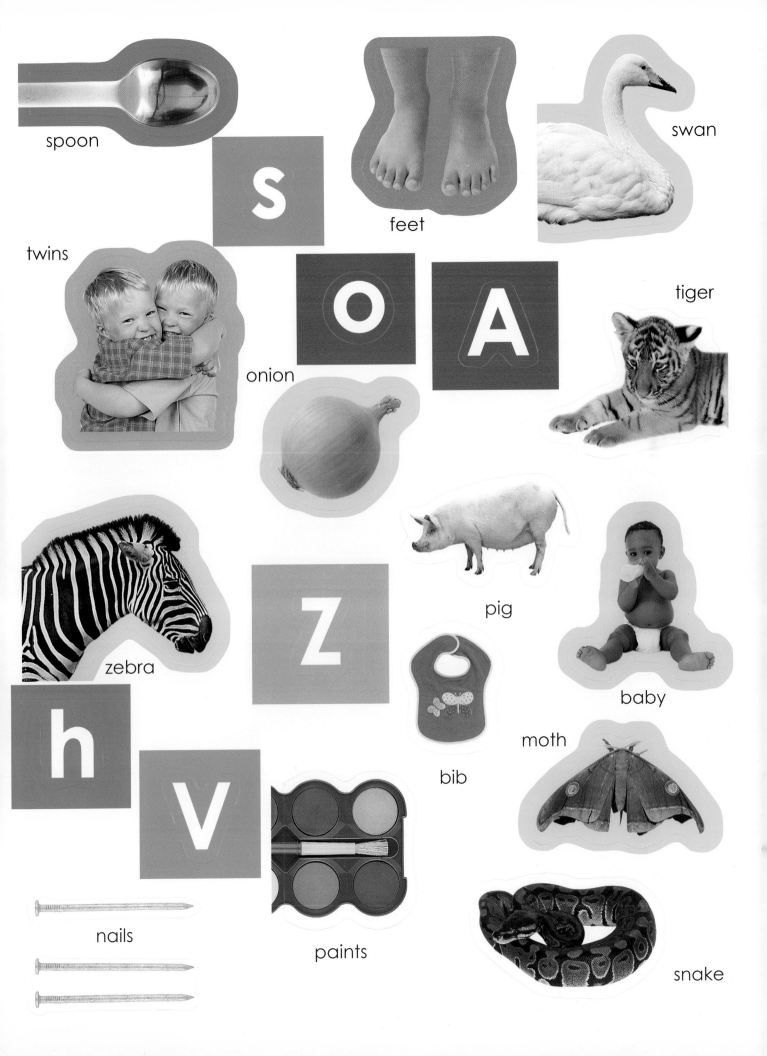

spoon

S

feet

swan

twins

O

A

tiger

onion

zebra

Z

pig

baby

h

bib

moth

V

nails

paints

snake

wheel

ABC stickers

elephant

wolf

tricycle

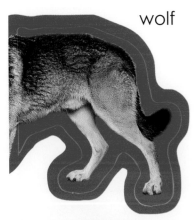

dinosaur

starfish

fox

quick

socks

watch

wheelbarrow

yo-yo

M

P

train

ABC stickers

violin

V

U

tiger

jacket

quiet

umbrella

orange

rose

t

nine

helicopter

G

swan

W

cup

box

I

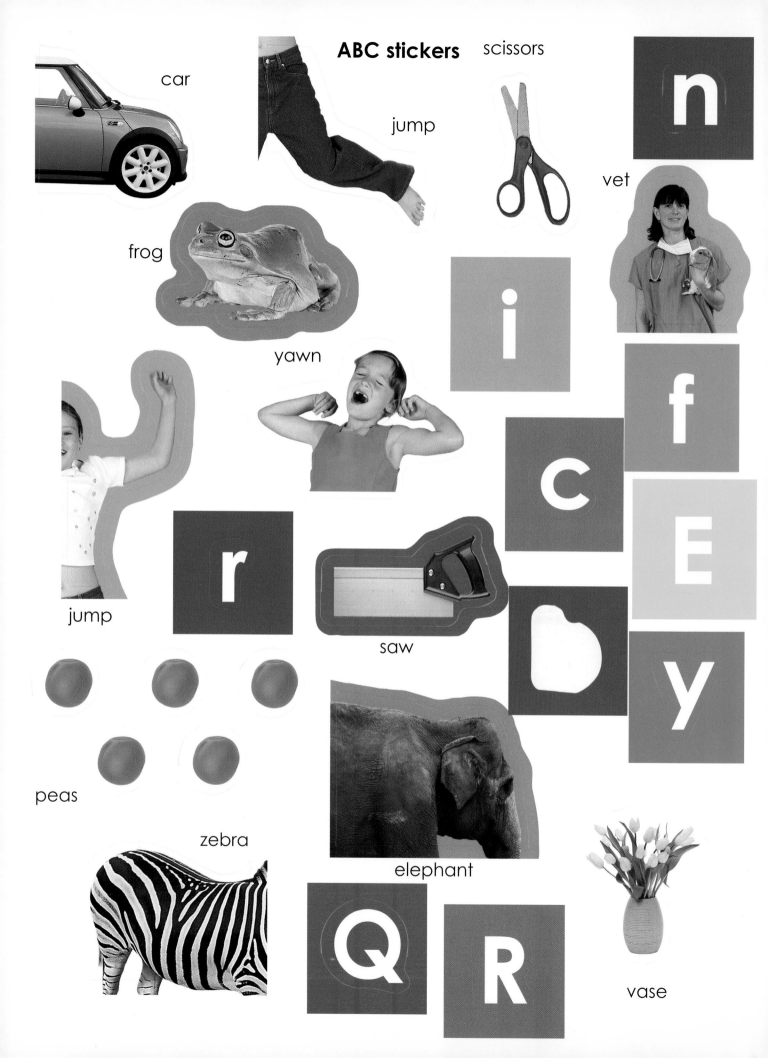

ABC stickers

car

jump

scissors

n

vet

frog

i

yawn

f

c

E

jump

r

saw

b

y

peas

elephant

zebra

Q

R

vase

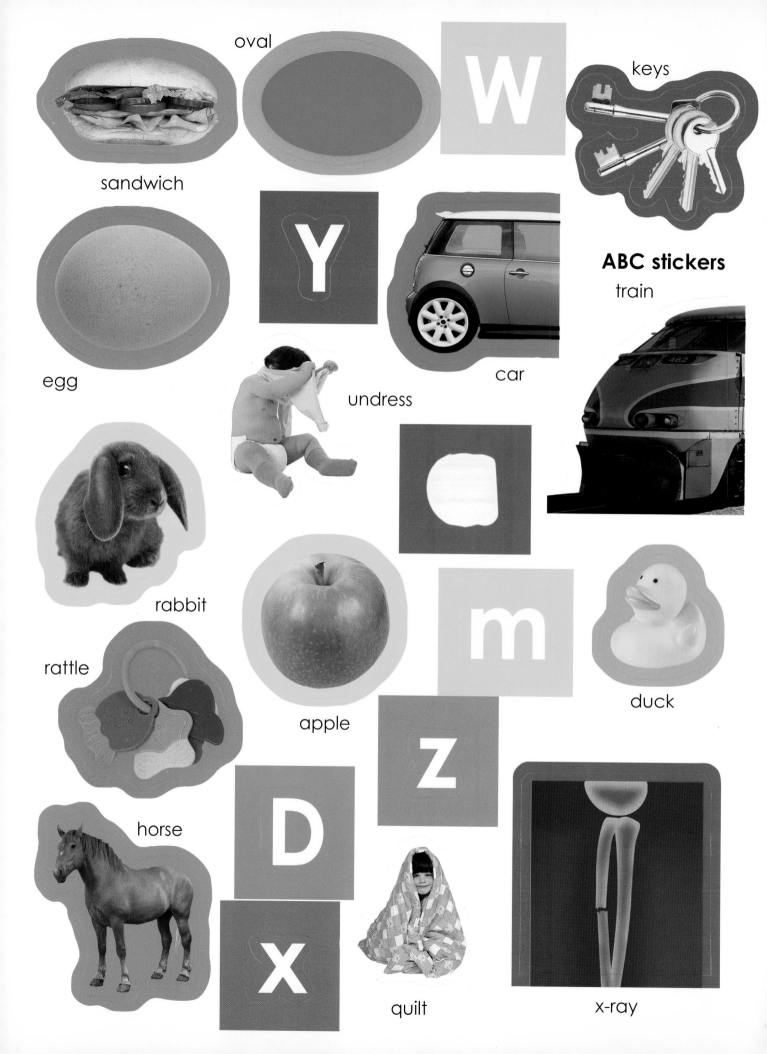

sandwich

oval

W

keys

egg

Y

car

ABC stickers

train

undress

rabbit

rattle

apple

m

duck

horse

Z

D

X

quilt

x-ray

Numbers stickers

present

hat

race car

orange

nine

bee

puppy

five

triangle

pencil

ostrich

boy

pepper

star

duck

coin

chicken

pumpkin

button

foal

fuel truck

grapes

popsicle

penguin

coin

chili

pencil

strawberry

girl

candy

tractor

snake

acorns

girl

boy

nine

balloon

yacht

button

boy

sheepdog

bear

pencil

button

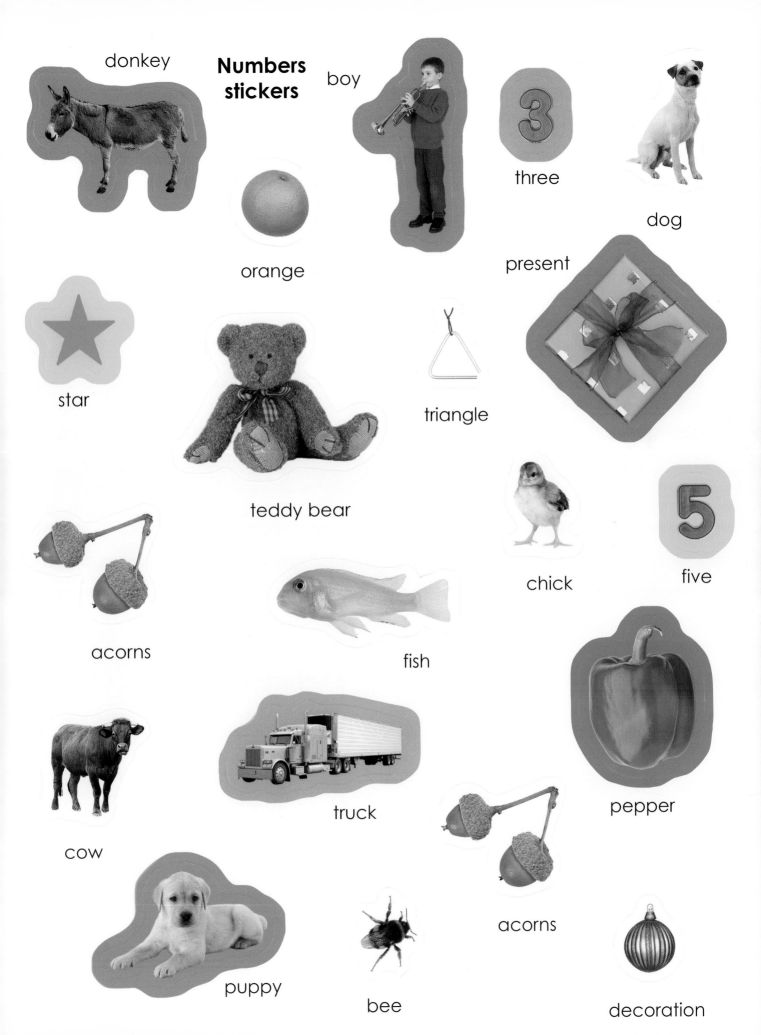

donkey

Numbers stickers

boy

three

dog

orange

present

star

teddy bear

triangle

chick

five

acorns

fish

cow

truck

pepper

acorns

puppy

bee

decoration

melon slice

button

Numbers stickers

decoration

pepper

hat

bee

banana

candy

race car

star

clock

ladybug

lemon

candy

fuel truck

three

ice cream

eggplant

dress

trains

penguin

triangle

chocolate
egg

chick

**Numbers
stickers**

flower

three

ladybug

donut

cupcake

frog

penguin

peas

t-shirt

candy

decoration

acorns

puppy

triangle

bug

girl

gift bow

pencil

cupcake

leaf

gift bow

snake

coin

pig

toucan

Numbers stickers

pencil

bug

nine

tomatoes

seven

star

triangle

cupcake

bucket

fish

ice cream

button

frog

bee

decoration

chick

yacht

penguin

t-shirt

present

fish

flower

**Numbers
stickers**

foal

candy

decoration

frog

die

fish

chick

coin

three

chick

toy duck

cupcake

bug

decoration

fish

chocolate
egg

fire truck

coin

duckling

cherry

puppy

five

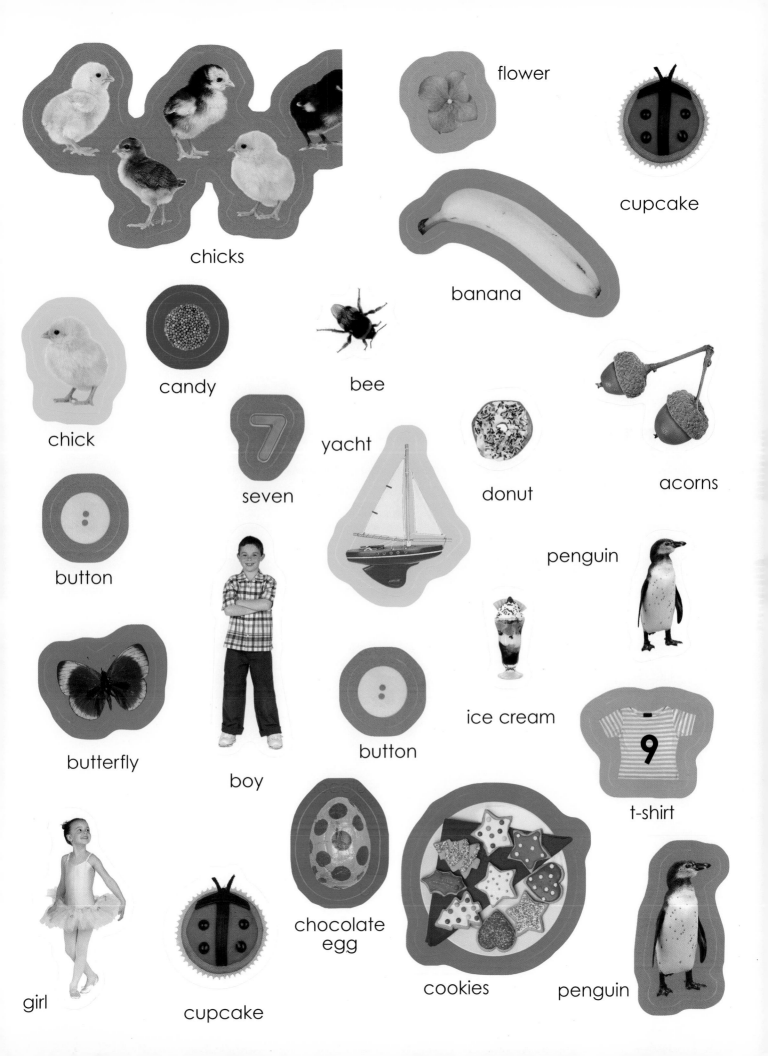

chicks

flower

cupcake

banana

candy

bee

chick

acorns

seven

yacht

donut

button

penguin

butterfly

ice cream

boy

button

t-shirt

girl

chocolate egg

cookies

penguin

cupcake

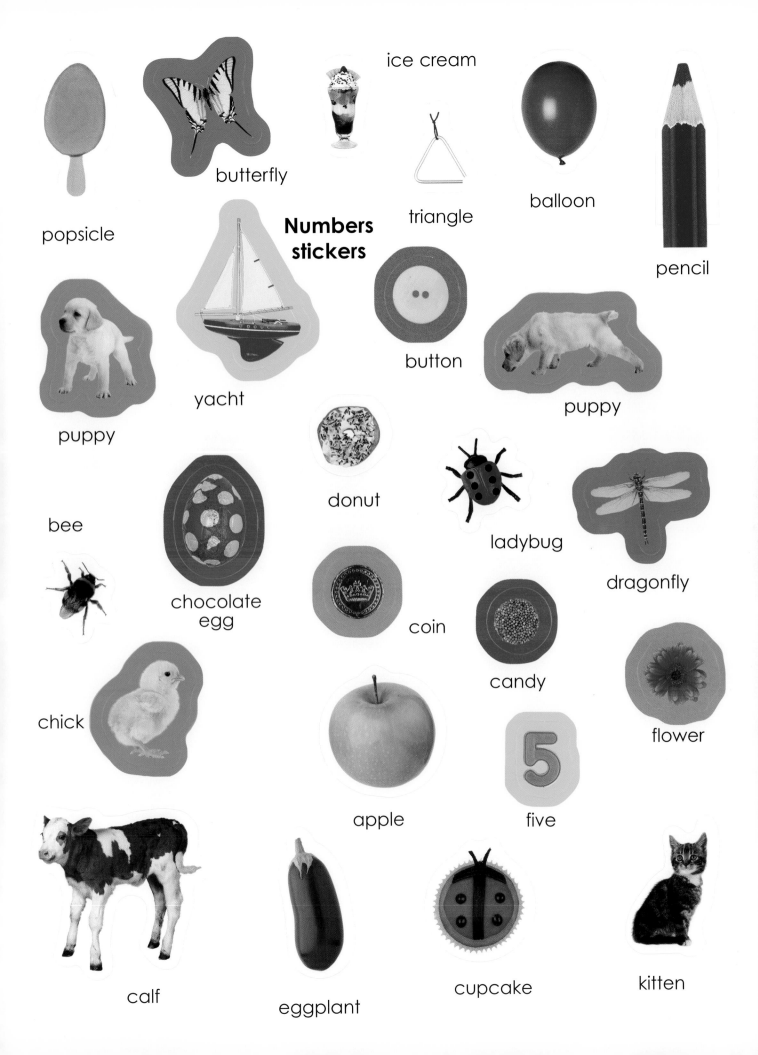

popsicle

butterfly

ice cream

triangle

balloon

pencil

Numbers stickers

puppy

yacht

button

puppy

bee

chocolate egg

donut

ladybug

dragonfly

coin

candy

chick

apple

five

flower

calf

eggplant

cupcake

kitten

three

digger

seven

butterfly

eggplant

dragonfly

donut

lamb

candy

chick

kitten

star

ice cream

five

horse

penguin

cupcake

kitten

candy

girl

nine

chocolate
egg

fish

octopus

dragonfly

girl

car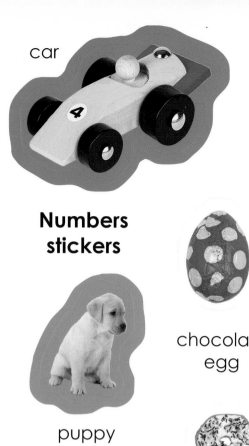

triangle

girl

chick

Numbers stickers

chocolate egg

chick

dress

bug

puppy

donut

pencil

five

one

kitten

bee

goldfish

one

gift bow

ice cream

sheep

chick

kitten

fish

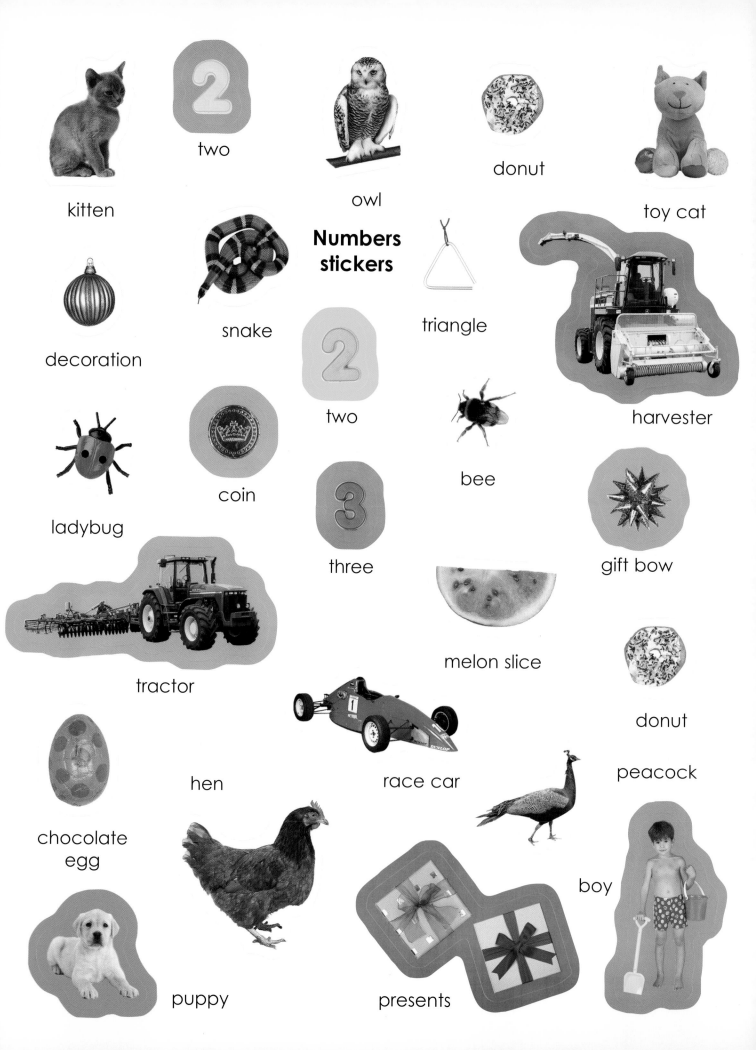

kitten

two

owl

donut

toy cat

decoration

snake

Numbers stickers

triangle

harvester

ladybug

coin

two

bee

gift bow

three

tractor

melon slice

donut

hen

race car

peacock

chocolate egg

boy

puppy

presents

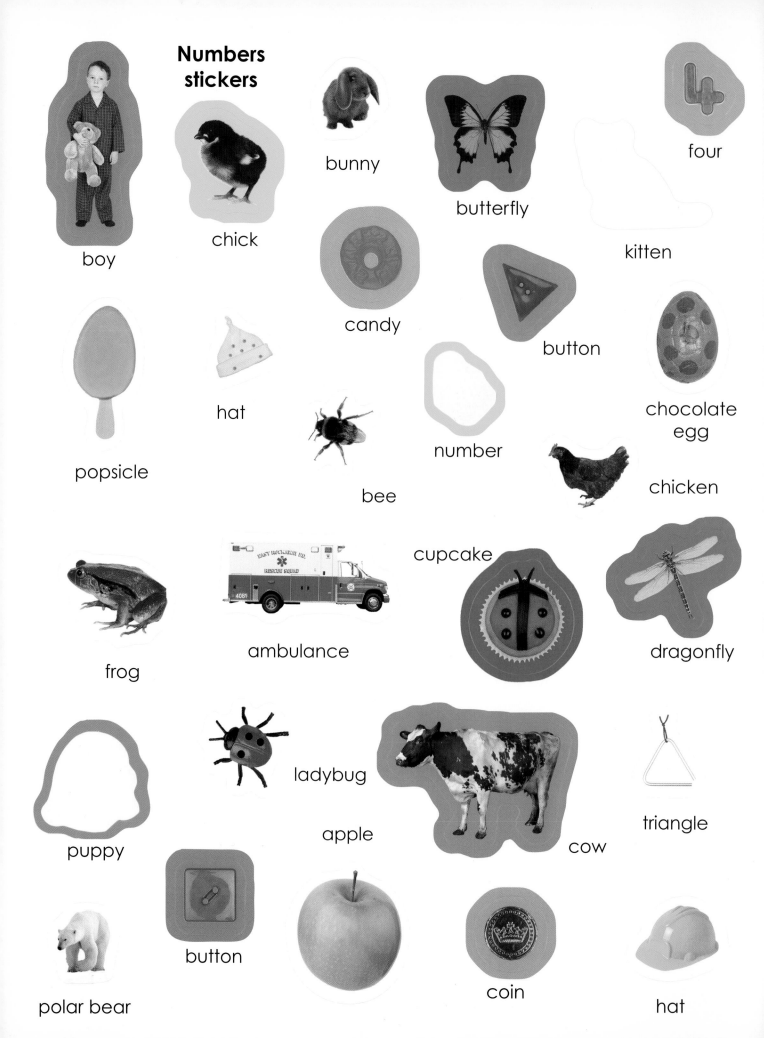

Numbers stickers

boy

chick

bunny

butterfly

four

kitten

candy

button

chocolate egg

popsicle

hat

bee

number

chicken

frog

ambulance

cupcake

dragonfly

puppy

ladybug

apple

cow

triangle

polar bear

button

apple

coin

hat

camel

hat

ostrich

five

chick

fuel truck

candy

dog

cherry

goat

hay bale

five

three

balloon

dog

lemon

dress

snake

candies

boy

frog

seven

ice cream

puppy

Colors stickers

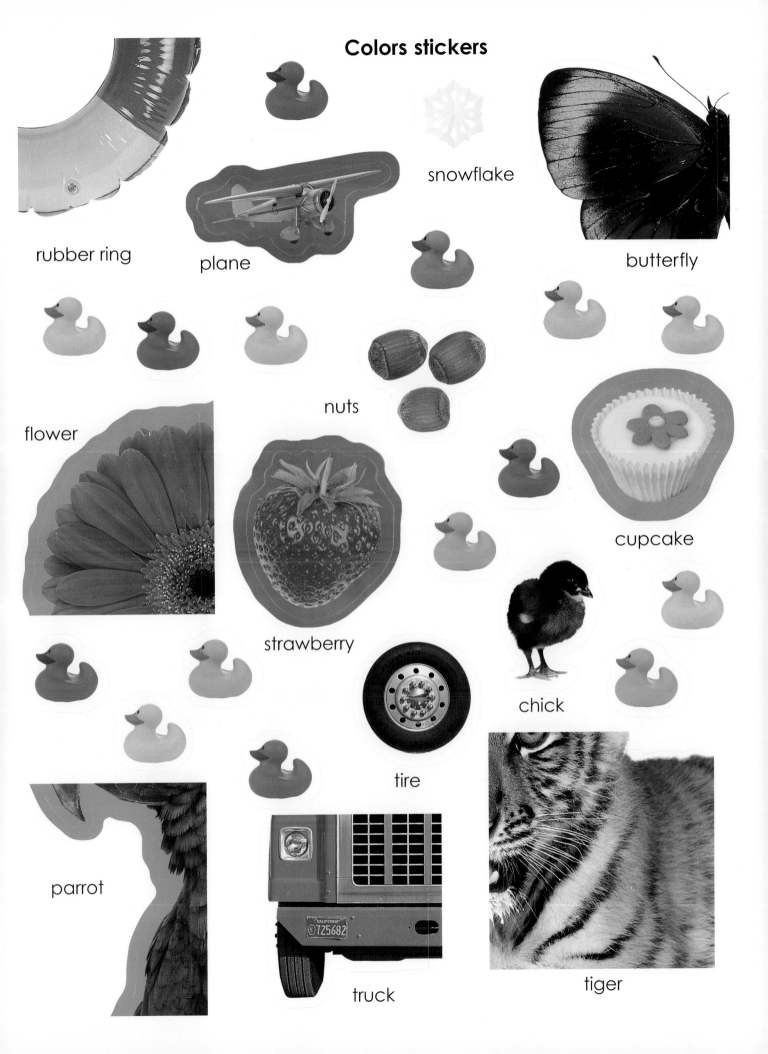

rubber ring

plane

snowflake

butterfly

nuts

flower

cupcake

strawberry

chick

parrot

tire

truck

tiger

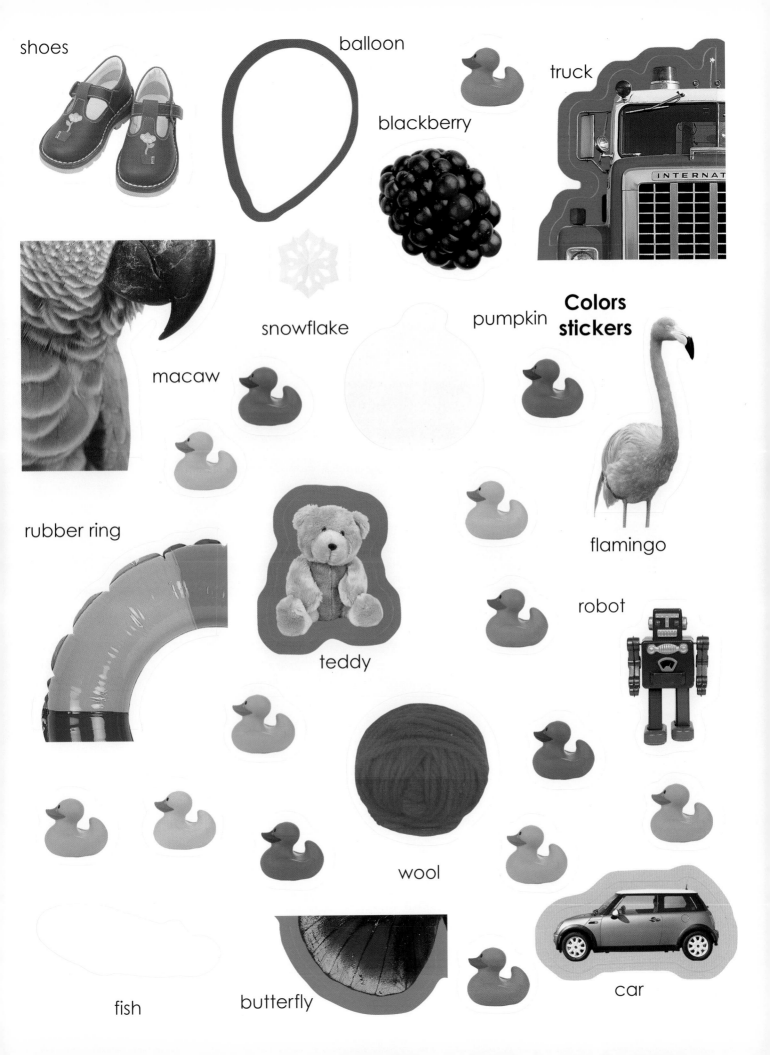

shoes

balloon

blackberry

truck

snowflake

macaw

pumpkin

Colors stickers

flamingo

rubber ring

teddy

robot

wool

fish

butterfly

car

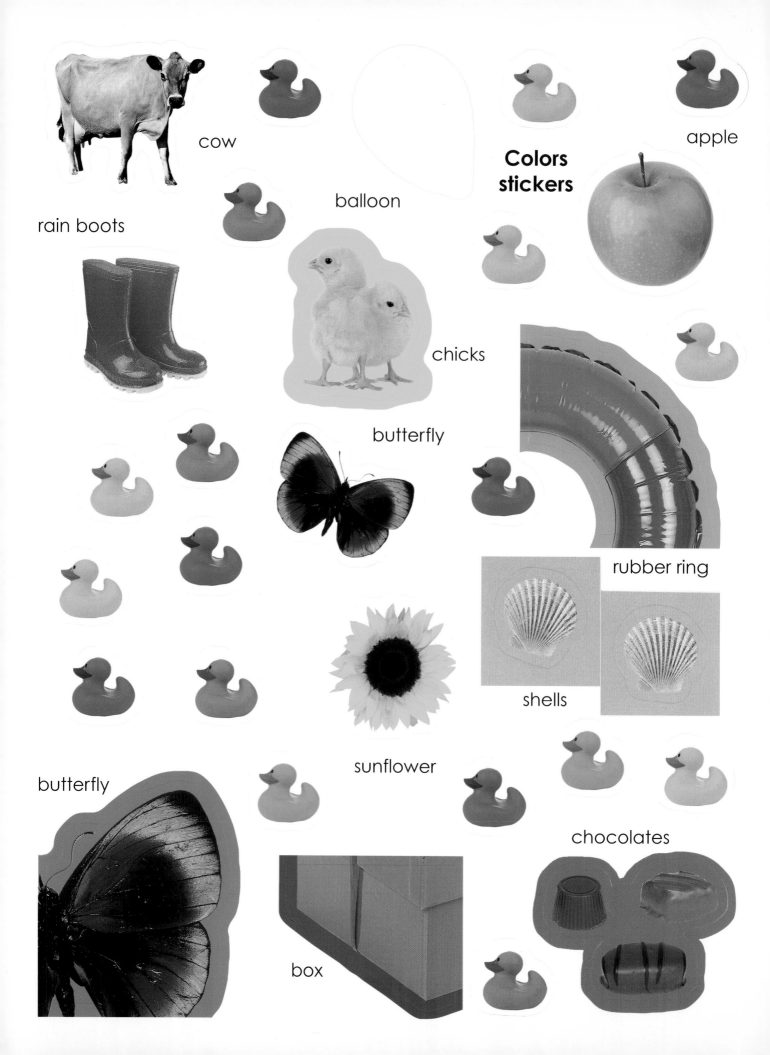

cow

balloon

Colors stickers

apple

rain boots

chicks

butterfly

rubber ring

shells

sunflower

butterfly

chocolates

box

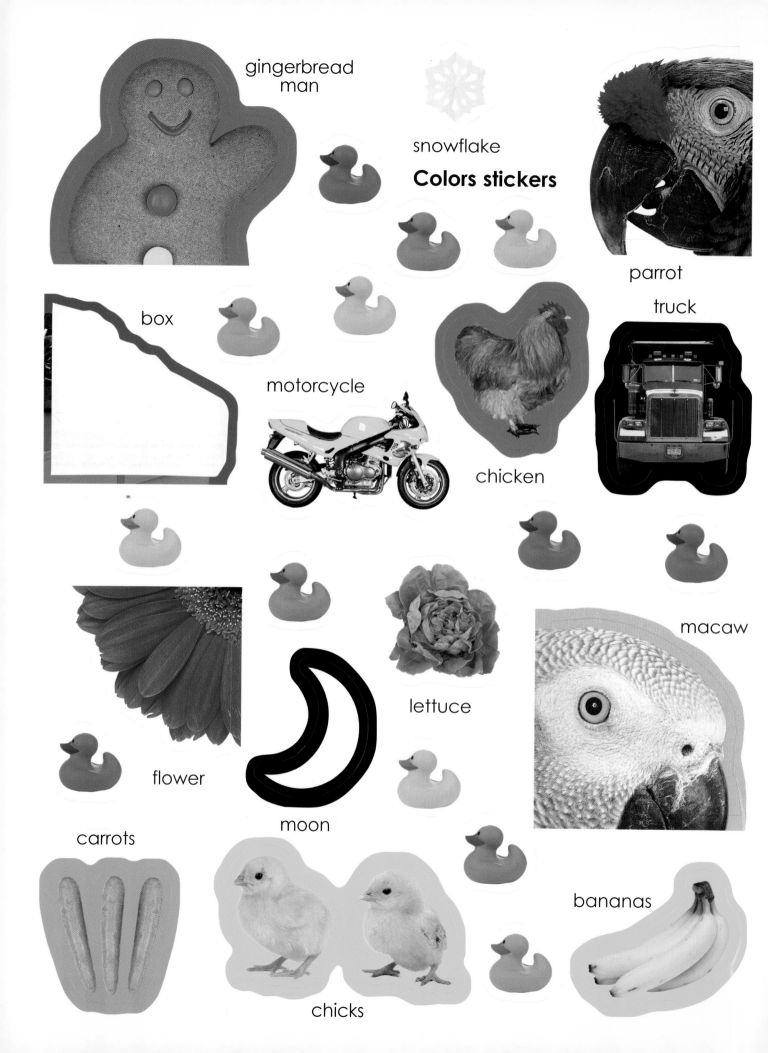

gingerbread man

snowflake

Colors stickers

parrot

truck

box

motorcycle

chicken

macaw

lettuce

flower

moon

carrots

chicks

bananas

truck

box

scissors

ant

frog

Colors stickers

candies

grapes

fish

snowflake

dog

glove

butterfly

night

parrot

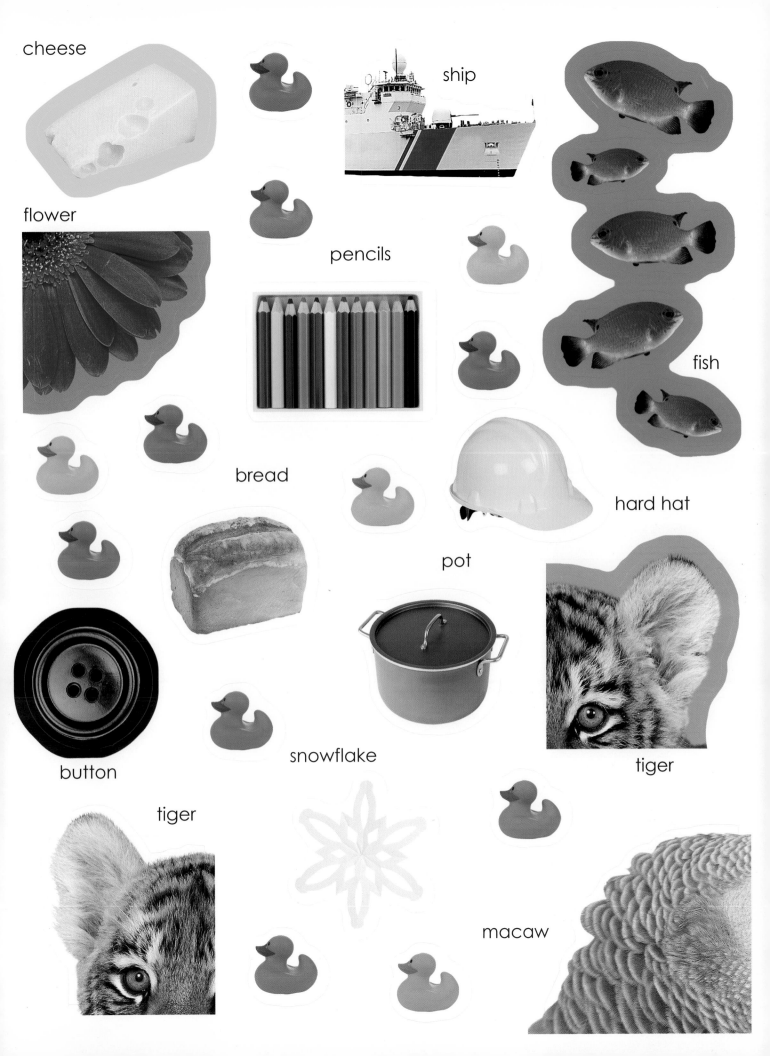

cheese

flower

ship

pencils

fish

bread

hard hat

pot

button

snowflake

tiger

tiger

macaw

sheep

boy

pig

Drawing stickers

horse

race car

butterfly

cow

puppy

chick

tortoise

truck

tractor

cyclist

chicken

fire engine

chick

lamb

car

wool

jeep

ambulance

bus

cow

Drawing stickers

goat

chick

dog

piglet

sheep

jet

puppy

train

rooster

puppy

truck

ladybug

boat

duckling

race car

dog

sheep

dog

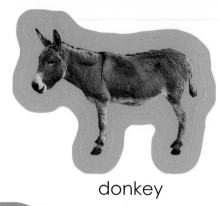

donkey

dog

lamb

Drawing stickers

concrete mixer

car

digger

honey

puppy

fish

puppy

bees

chick

motorcycle

plane

truck

pick-up truck

helicopter

milk

dog

bus

dog

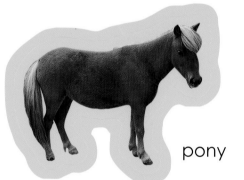

van

duck

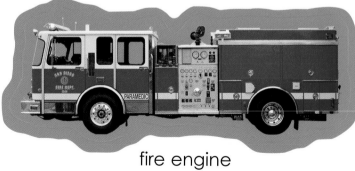

puppy

chick

train

Drawing stickers

pony

delivery truck

flower

fire engine

egg

car

dump truck

These stickers are just for fun.
You can stick them
wherever you like!

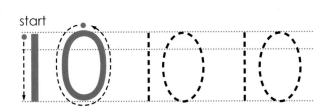

start

10 10 10 10

candies

donuts

chocolate eggs

ten ten ten

How many ice creams do you need to make ten?

How many
brown animals are there?

How many number '10' race cars are there?

Find the stickers and write the big numbers.

How many things are there altogether?

Find the ducks and stick them on the

Count the ducks and write the answers in the boxes.

How many
red ducks?

How many
green ducks?

How many
yellow ducks?

How many
blue ducks?

How many red
and green ducks?

How many blue
and yellow ducks?

How many ducks
are there on
this page?

How many ducks
are there
altogether?

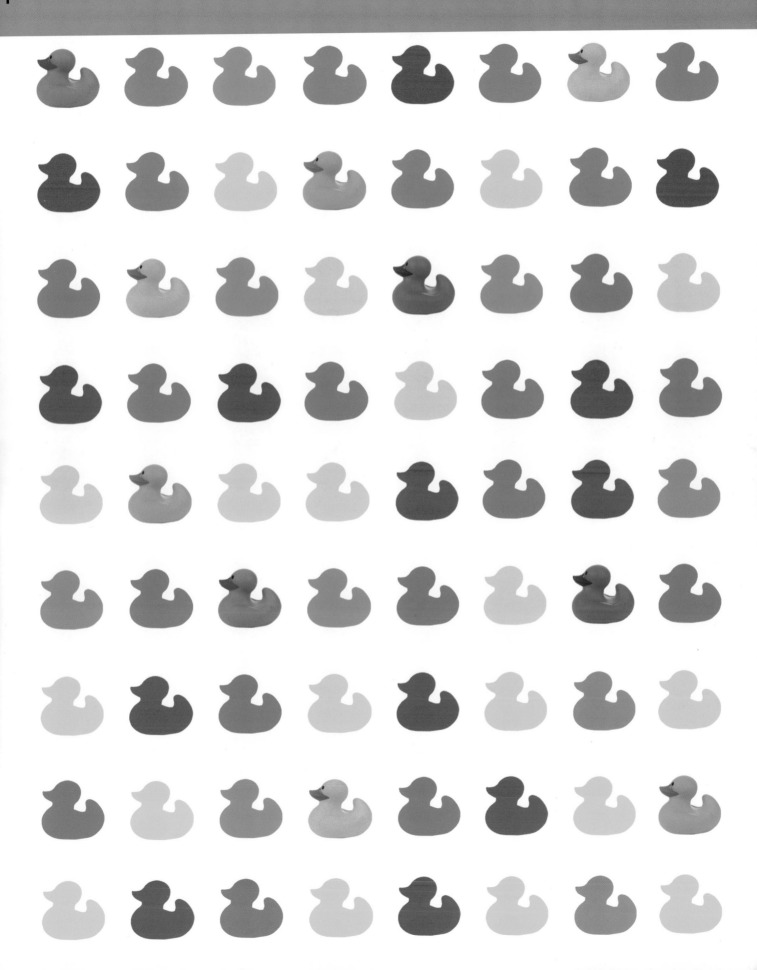

Red

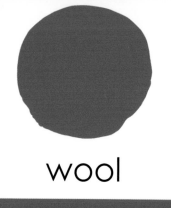

wool

truck

strawberry

plane

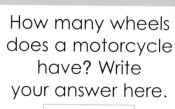

shoes

Yellow

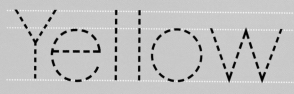

sunflower

bananas

motorcycle

How many wheels does a motorcycle have? Write your answer here.

cheese

scissors

chicks

Blue

butterflies

robot

Can you count how many fish there are? Write your answer here.

fish

Orange

pumpkin

carrots

Can you count how many carrots there are? Write your answer here.

glove

tiger

Green

lettuce

frog

What fruit can be red or green? Write your answer here.

apple

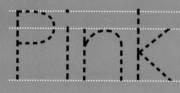
parrot

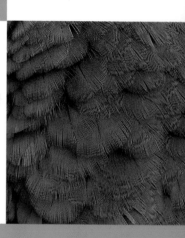

Pink

flamingo

flower

cupcake

rain boots

Brown

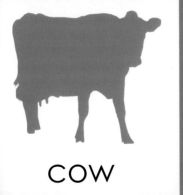

cow

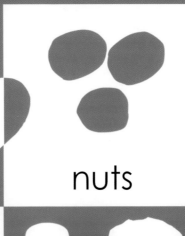

nuts

chicken

teddy

gingerbread
man

chocolates

bread

Purple

balloons

Can you count
how many balloons
there are? Write
your answer here.

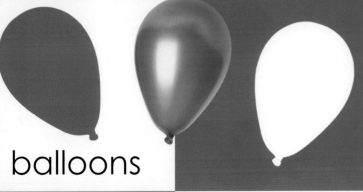

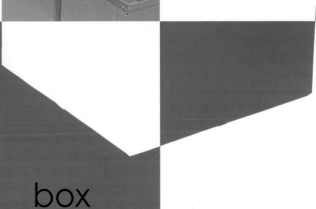

grapes

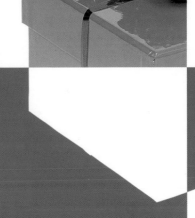

box

Black

tire

truck

chick

button

night

blackberry

Can you count how many stars there are? Write your answer here.

ant

White

snowflakes

hard hat

dog

moon

ship

Gray

macaw

fish

car

shells

pot

Multi-colored

rubber ring

candies

Can you count how many candies there are? Write your answer here.

rainbow

pencils

Dogs

dog

Look

Trace

d

Write and draw

puppy

Look

Trace

p

Write and draw

Counting

Write the number of dogs in this box. ☐

Write the number of puppies in this box. ☐

Cars

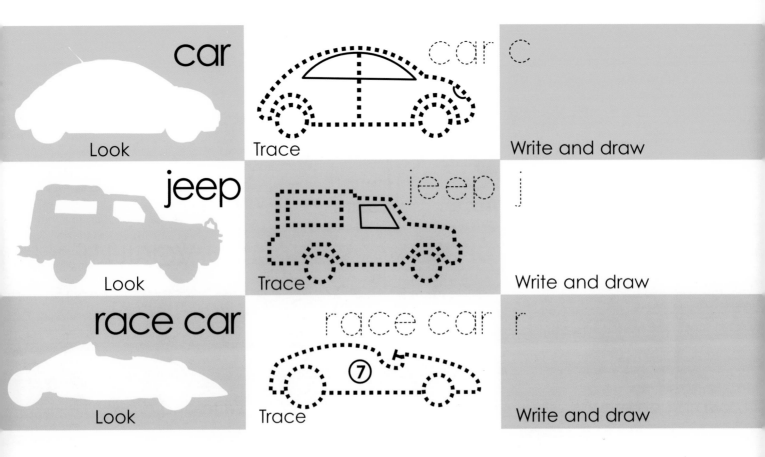

car

Look

Trace

car c

Write and draw

jeep

Look

Trace

jeep j

Write and draw

race car

Look

Trace

race car r

Write and draw

Spot the difference

Find the stickers and circle the differences on the pictures.

truck

motorcycle

Farm babies

duckling

Look

duckling

Trace

d

Write and draw

piglet

Look

piglet

Trace

p

Write and draw

Sorting

Write the letters that these animal names begin with.

donkey

goose

sheep

Circle all of the lambs.

Circle the identical chicks.

Trucks

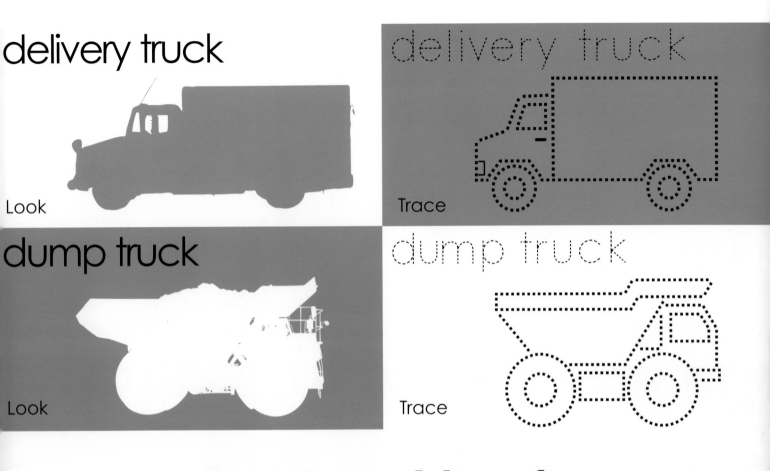

delivery truck

Look

delivery truck

Trace

dump truck

Look

dump truck

Trace

Front and back

Find the stickers and draw the other halves of these machines.

train

boat

car

truck

On the farm

COW

Look

cow

Trace

c

Write and draw

sheep

Look

sheep

Trace

s

Write and draw

Matching

Find the stickers and match the animals to the things that they make.

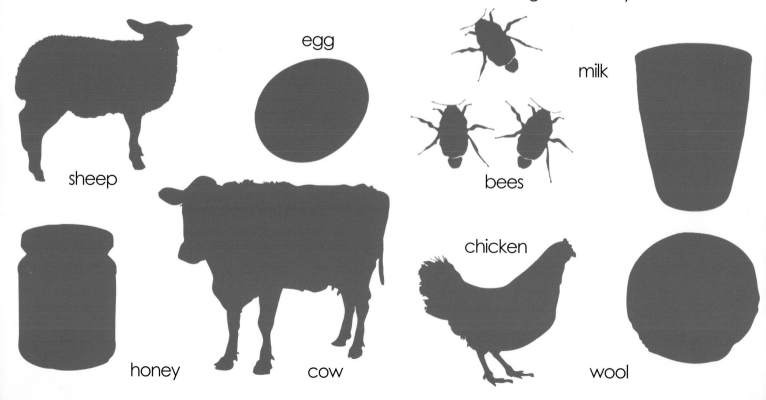

sheep

egg

milk

bees

honey

cow

chicken

wool

On the farm

tractor

Look

tractor

Trace

pick-up truck

Look

pick-up truck

Trace

Missing letters

Find the stickers and complete the missing letters in these words.

 c a r

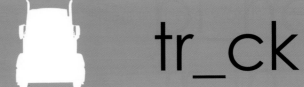 tr_in

b u s

 tr_ck

 v a n

pl_ne

 j e t

 digg_r

Horses

horse

Look

horse

Trace

h

Write and draw

pony

Look

pony

Trace

p

Write and draw

Heads and tails

Find the stickers and finish drawing these animal pictures.

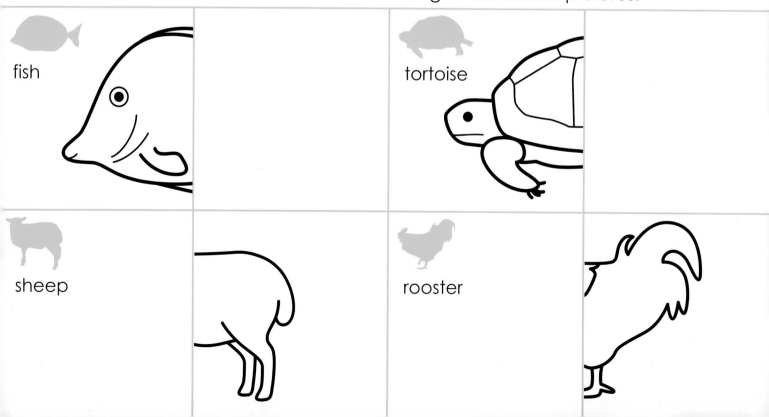

fish

tortoise

sheep

rooster

Emergency

fire engine
Look

fire engine
Trace

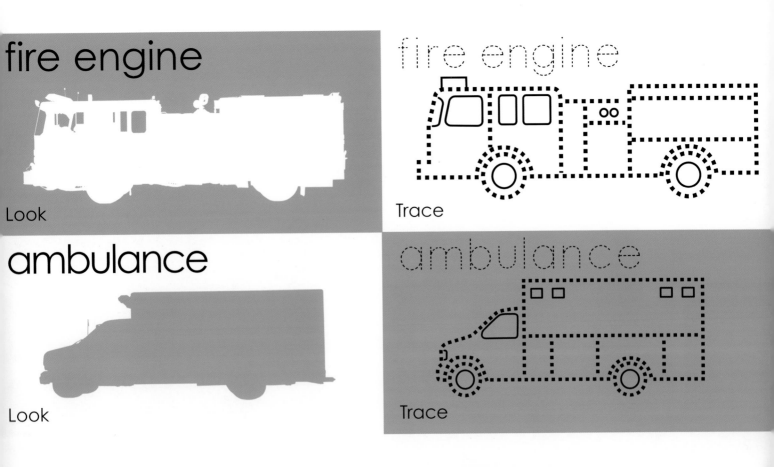

ambulance
Look

ambulance
Trace

Follow the lines

Find the vehicle stickers and trace over the lines to take the people to them.

pilot

helicopter

firefighter

fire engine

construction worker

concrete mixer

racing driver

race car

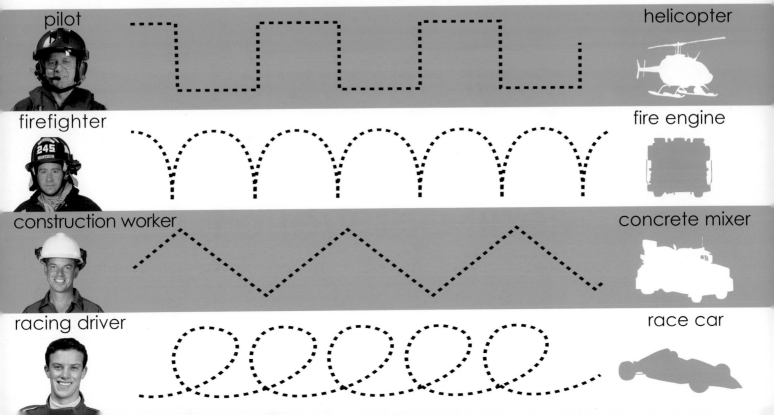

Bugs

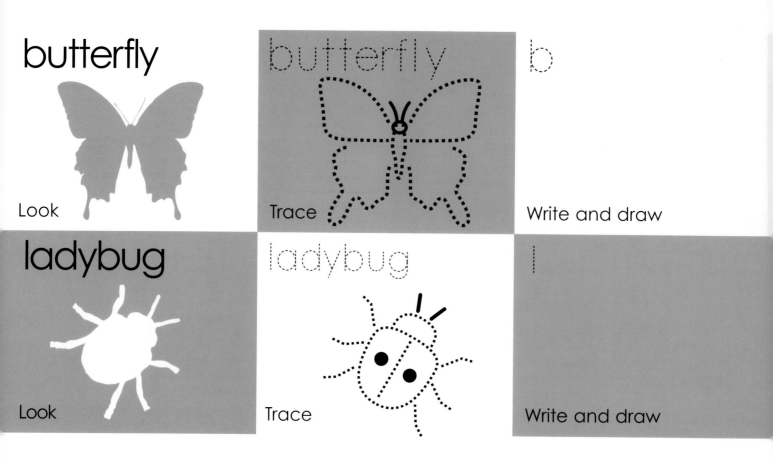

butterfly

Look

butterfly

Trace

b

Write and draw

ladybug

Look

ladybug

Trace

l

Write and draw

Bee maze

Find the flower sticker and help lead the bees to it.

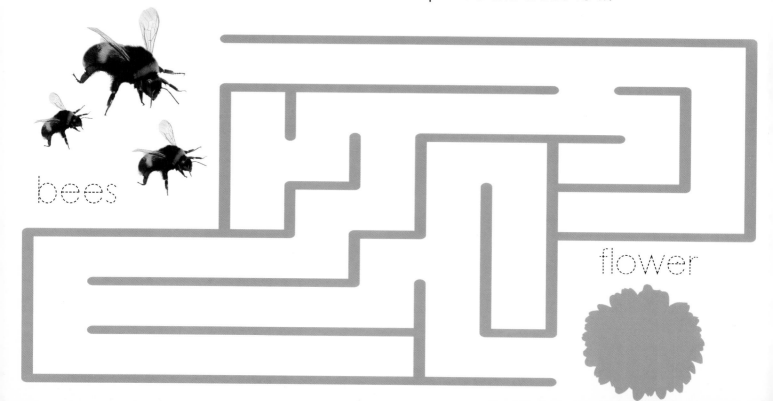

bees

flower

Two wheels

How to draw a bicycle.

Draw two circles for the wheels.

Draw the frame and handlebars.

Finish with the saddle and pedals.

Now try to draw one by yourself.

Follow the lines

Find the stickers and get the bus, the boy and the cyclist to school.

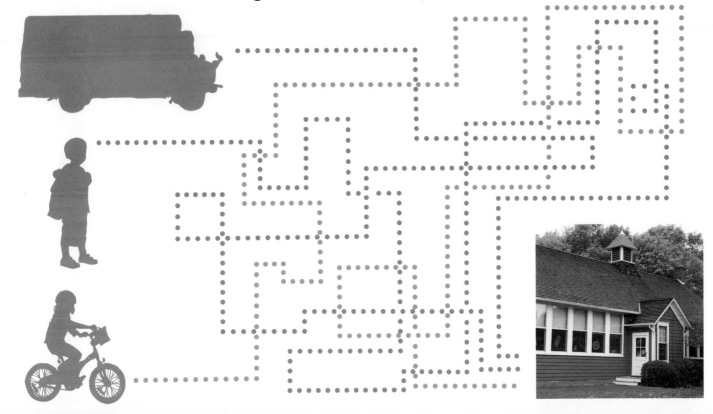

Dot to dot

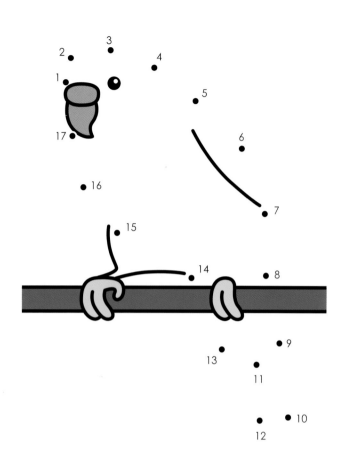

Do you know which animals these are?

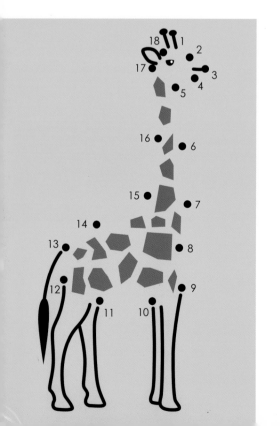

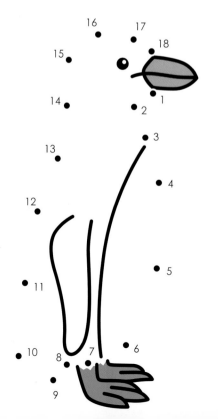

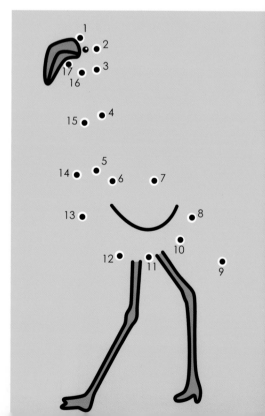

Dot to dot

What are the names of these things that go?

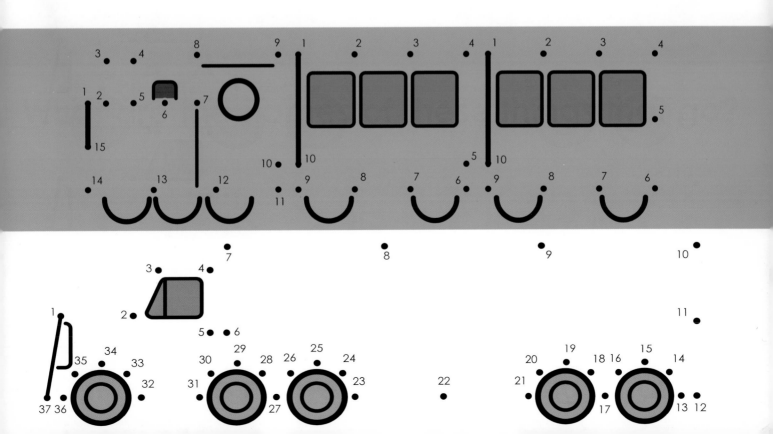

Circle the number of vegetables in each box, then do the activities below.

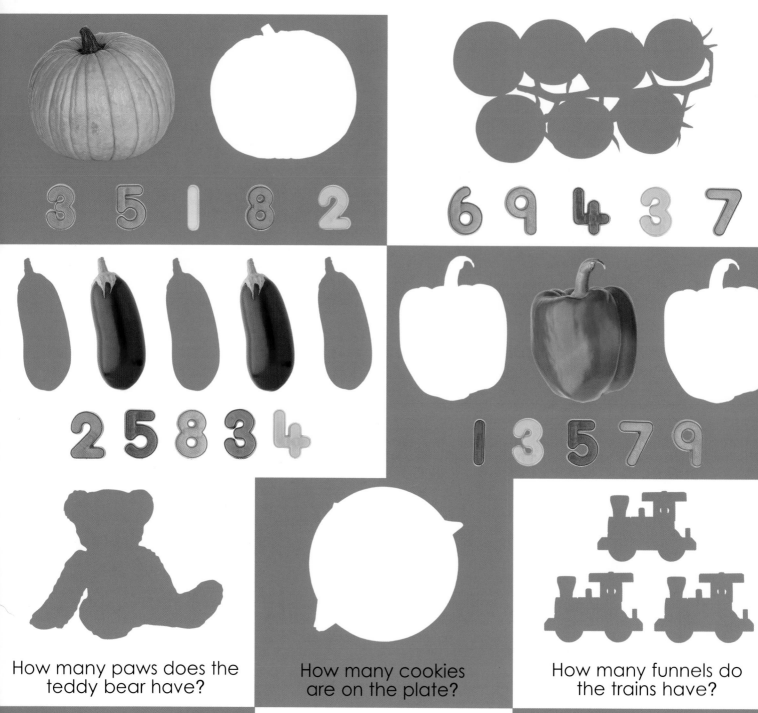

3 5 1 8 2   6 9 4 3 7

2 5 8 3 4   1 3 5 7 9

How many paws does the teddy bear have?

How many cookies are on the plate?

How many funnels do the trains have?

How many spots does the die have?

How many petals does the flower have?

How many wheels does the race car have?